Affirmations for Mindful Leaders

Jessica R. Dreistadt

Affirmations for Mindful Leaders

© 2013, 2016 Jessica R. Dreistadt.

All rights reserved. No part of this publication may be reproduced, distributed, or transmitted in any form or by any means, including photocopying, recording, or other electronic or mechanical methods, without the prior written permission of the publisher, except in the case of brief quotations embodied in critical reviews and certain other noncommercial uses permitted by copyright law. Requests for permission to use or reproduce material from this book should be directed to utopia@fruitioncoalition.com.

ISBN 978-1535470483

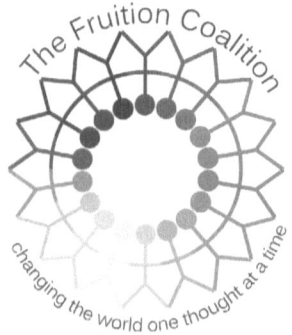

The Fruition Coalition
Lehigh Valley, PA
www.fruitioncoalition.com
www.jessicardreistadt.com

Introduction

Affirmations are brief statements that can be used to help leaders:

- clarify their true purpose;
- focus their attention;
- expand their self-awareness;
- mobilize their energy;
- inspire them toward positive action;
- connect their dreams with reality;
- improve their effectiveness; and
- increase their work and life satisfaction.

This book contains 50 affirmations for leaders who are mindful, ethical, intentional, authentic, and transformational. The affirmations span ten areas: vision; purpose; passion; power; relation-ships; innovation; risk; responsibility; balance; and transformation. Each affirmation has been carefully designed to help leaders feel more motivated, inspired, purposeful, and connect-ed.

There are several ways that you can use this book. You can:
- read it from beginning to end;
- read through a section that reflects your needs or interests;
- choose an affirmation as the focus of a prayer or meditation;
- use an affirmation to carefully reflect on your actions as a leader;
- draw or write on each of the affirmation pages to capture your related thoughts and feelings;

- use an affirmation as a prompt for journaling or discussion; and/or
- place affirmations that deeply resonate with you in places where you will frequently see them.

You may like some affirmations more than others. You may find that some have little meaning for you. I encourage you to use those that are aligned with your leadership practice and ignore those that do not. At the end of each section, there is also a place for you to write your own affirmations to reflect your unique ideas about leadership.

With best wishes for mindful leadership,

Jessica R. Dreistadt

Vision

I am excited about the possibilities I envision for the future.

My vision for the future is beautiful and miraculous.

My vision for the future is an expression of my true life purpose and values.

I openly share my vision for the future with others.

I am realizing my vision through my work every day.

My Vision Affirmations:

Purpose

I cherish all of the many gifts that have been entrusted to me.

My work is meaningful and significant.

My work is consistently an expression of my most brilliant life purpose.

All of my thoughts, words, and actions reflect my life purpose.

I wake up each morning eager to pursue my life purpose.

My Purpose Affirmations:

Passion

I am passionate and excited about my work.

My passion is contagious.

I am profoundly in touch with my deepest desires.

My passions guide my priorities.

My passions are fully integrated into my work and life.

My Passion Affirmations:

Power

I am in touch with my source of personal power.

My power is immensely beautiful.

I appreciate the immense power within every person's heart, mind, and spirit.

I freely share my power with others.

I use my power to create a better world.

My Power Affirmations:

Relationships

I care deeply about the impact my leadership has on others.

I authentically involve others in my leadership.

I feel good about serving and seeking assistance from others.

I trust my co-workers and colleagues.

My relationships reflect my spiritual and ethical values.

My Relationship Affirmations:

Innovation

I am creative and innovative.

I crave novelty and whimsy.

My imagination is magnificent.

I love to play with ideas and possibilities.

I have the ability to create my visions and dreams.

My Innovation Affirmations:

Risk

My confidence and faith in myself and in the world create a strong sense of internal security.

I am courageous and brave.

I thrive when I feel vulnerable.

I encourage others to make mistakes.

I joyfully release the outcomes of my leadership.

My Risk Affirmations:

Responsibility

I am consistently honest and dependable.

I accept responsibility for my mistakes.

I honor my intentions and promises.

I deserve trust and respect.

My leadership is open and responsive.

My Responsibility Affirmations:

Balance

I take good care of my body, mind, and soul.

I make time for myself, my family, and my friends.

I radiate positive energy.

My life is peaceful and harmonious.

I am happy and fulfilled.

My Balance Affirmations:

Transformation

I am excited by the possibilities of personal, organizational, and social transformation.

All of my thoughts, words, and actions profoundly influence the world.

I appreciate the complexity of change.

My leadership has an immeasurable impact.

I am a phenomenal leader.

I am happy and fulfilled.

My Transformation Affirmations:

Notes

www.ingramcontent.com/pod-product-compliance
Lightning Source LLC
Chambersburg PA
CBHW021440170526
45164CB00001B/326